AUG - 1996

THINGS
THAT
HAPPEN
ONCE

Poetry by Rodney Jones

THINGS
THAT
HAPPEN
ONCE

new poems

RODNEY JONES

Houghton Mifflin Company

Boston   New York   1996

For information about permission to reproduce selections from this book,
write to Permissions, Houghton Mifflin Company, 215 Park Avenue South,
New York, New York 10003.

For information about this and other Houghton Mifflin trade and reference
books and multimedia products, visit The Bookstore at Houghton Mifflin
on the World Wide Web at http://www.hmco.com/trade/.

Library of Congress Cataloging-in-Publication Data
Jones, Rodney, date.
   Things that happen once : new poems / Rodney Jones.
      p. cm.
   ISBN 0-395-77143-9
   I. Title.
   PS3560.O5263T45   1996   95-44941
   811'.54 — dc20   CIP

Printed in the United States of America
QUM 10 9 8 7 6 5 4 3 2 1

Book design by Melodie Wertelet

Acknowledgment is made to the editors of the publications in which earlier versions of
the following poems originally appeared:

"After Workshop" and "For My Sister" in *The American Poetry Review;* "Beautiful
Child," "First Coca-Cola," "On Pickiness," and "TV" in *The Atlantic Monthly;* "All My
Children," "Bread," "Country Heroism," "Don't Worry," "The End of Communism,"
"Lurleen," "The Plan for World Government," "A Ride with the Commander," and
"Risks" in *The Black Warrior Review;* "The Consolations of Poetry" and "Mink" in
Boulevard; "Dirty Blues" in *Crazyhorse;* "My Father's Memory" and "Nell" in *The
Georgia Review;* "Waking Up" in *Grand Street;* "Hunger" and "On Censorship" in *The
New Orleans Review;* "The Pass" and "A Slide of the Ladies Home Missionary Society
Meeting" in *Parnassus;* "An Errand for My Grandmother," "First Space Travelers," and
"Mortal Sorrows" in *Poetry;* "Filling the Gully" and "First Fraudulent Muse" in *Poetry
Northwest;* "Letters from the Earth," "A Prayer to the Goddess," and "Sex" in *Quarterly
West;* "Ground Sense" in *Shenandoah;* "Indian Turnip," "In the Spirit of Limuel
Hardin," "Perfection," and "The Troubles That Women Start Are Men" in *The Southern
Review.*

Several of these poems first appeared or were reprinted in *The Troubles That Women
Start Are Men,* a signed, limited edition published in 1995 by Parallel Editions of
Tuscaloosa, Alabama.

For Gloria

Contents

The asters speak
out of a world of change, of repetition,
for those events that only happen once.

— Peter Davison

I.

Last Myths
of the Pioneers

TV

All the preachers claimed it was Satan.
Now the first sets seem more venerable
Than Abraham or Williamsburg
Or the avant-garde. Back then nothing,

Not even the bomb, had ever looked so new.
It seemed almost heretical watching it
When we visited relatives in the city,
Secretly delighting, but saying later,

After church, probably it would not last,
It would destroy things: standards
And the sacredness of words in books.
It was well into the age of color,

Korea and Little Rock long past,
Before anyone got one. Suddenly some
Of them in the next valley had one.
You would know them by their lights

Burning late at night, and the recentness
And distance of events entering their talk,
But not one in our valley; for a long time
No one had one, so when the first one

Arrived in the van from the furniture store
And the men had set the box on the lawn,
At first we stood back from it, circling it
As they raised its antenna and staked in

The guy wires before taking it in the door,
And I seem to recall a kind of blue light
Flickering from inside and then a woman
Calling out that they had got it tuned in —

A little fuzzy, a ghost picture, but something
That would stay with us, the way we hurried
Down the dirt road, the stars, the silence,
Then everyone disappearing into the houses.

Mortal Sorrows

The tortures of lumbago consumed Aunt Madge,
And Leah Vest, once resigned from schoolmarming,
Could not be convinced to leave the house.
Mrs. Mary Hogan, after birthing her fifth son,

Lay bedfast for the last fifty-two years of her life,
Reporting shooting pains that would begin
High in her back and shear downward to her feet,
As though, she said, she had been glazed in lightning;

Also men, broken on bridges and mills,
Shell-shocked veterans, religious alcoholics —
Leldon Kilpatrick, Johnson Suggs, Whitey Carlyle:
They came and sat there too, leafing through

Yellowing *Pageant*s and *Progressive Farmer*s;
One by one, all entered in and talked,
While the good doctor gargled a dark chaff
In his pipe and took down symptoms,

Annotating them on his hidden chart —
Numbness, neuralgia, the knotted lymph,
The clammy palms — and then he'd scratch
His temple's meaningful patch of white

And scrawl out his unfailing barbiturate prescription
To be filled by his pharmacist brother-in-law
Until half the county had gathered as in a lap,
The quantum ache, the mutiny in every house.

How much pain, how many diseases
Consigned to the mythological, the dropped
Ovaries, the torn-up nerves, what women
Said, what men wanted to believe? Part of it

Laughable, I know. Still I want someone
To see, now that they lie safe in graves
Beyond the vacant stores, that someone
Listened and, hearing the wrong at the heart,

Named it something that sounded real, whatever
They lived through and died of. I remember
Mrs. Lyle, who called it a thorn in the flesh,
And Mr. Appleton, who had no roof in his mouth.

The Cycles of Silence

Before there were words, the sounds
Were already here. The meanings
Set down in books were already old
When the first brief lifetimes sparked

Hot in the cold salt battery of the sea.
Arrogant athlete, the obsolete god
Of nature, stands above it all, looking
Like Charlton Heston in *El Cid.*

He can't read the pages he turns,
Summer evenings and falling leaves.
And all that's been said dries with print.
And all that's been written is a kind

Of prayer to a god who no longer exists.
Our nature's the city in the spring,
Our newly inked dollars, the pollen
We buzz to carry through the streets

At the hour when the shops pinken
Like the petals of a stone blossom.
And still we arrive in late May
At the shingle cottage, throw open

The windows, sleep the sleep of things
That have been shut for a long time,
And, grunting and carping, wake,
Go out with first sun and return

With last sun, trim the white flesh
From the bluefish we have caught,
And eat them, sitting on the deck,
Above the raw cartilage of the surf.

The moon dawns with that look
Of an idiot mother gone to seed.
The old couple from next door,
Having made love for the first time

Since 1987, come tripping giddily
Across the sandburs, light beside us
With their lawn chairs and Chablis —
Just as we're ready for sleep,

He's starting to talk — trash bonds,
Grandkids, sports, the land yacht
They sail each year from Omaha
Docked under their cottage like a loaf —

Until his dreamboat pinches his cheek —
"Am I rich?" he asks. "He's rich," she
Says, "but what he really wanted
Was to write high drama for radio."

A great sadness, but you can see joy
In telling it, so later, when I'd meant
To be thinking of what there is
In the cycles of silence that renews us,

The women are in bed; he's Norm,
I'm Rod; we're staggering down
The surf toward the lighthouse. See,
He's got this big jelly glass of bourbon —

It's amber in the light from the jetty —
It's simple. He's happy. Then he's sad.
One moment, he's lifting it in a toast
To the Boston Braves and Archibald MacLeish —

But now he doesn't want it. It's not
The moment when he says, "Fuck it,"
And dumps it, but just afterward,
When he stands with the empty glass,

Wanting it again and knowing it lost,
But reaching down anyway — and this
Is when it's not language — it's whiskey,
And then it's the ocean in his mouth.

Last Myths of the Pioneers

Just as the date holds still before the day,
The main highway waited for years
After it was first leveled and paved,
And then there were just a few cars,

But the doctors still came in carriages,
And the wagons still rumbled house
To house with big blocks of ice
Nestled in sawdust under the tarpaulins

When Roosevelt closed the banks
And tanks rolled forward from the Third Reich.
It must have happened so gradually
That no one had noticed until one day

The oaks were moving east in the traffic
Beside them. The bears were gone,
And the last panther had vanished
When the truck slammed into the bridge.

Among flames whirling up through
The floorboard's dappling rust,
The old man found the driver, pinned
At the knee, but did not have the guts

To swing the ax. He would not hear
Of it again, although it would be
The one story that did not change
When the lights had spread everywhere

And the news flew in from the distance,
Blotting accents out. Even when
The freeway came, leaving that hill alone
Above the creek, and the house

Where the old man lived with no water
And lights, someone would tell me.
I think it was Clyde Appleton, who
Also had it that man-eating catfish swarmed

The bottomless hole in the river bend;
If not Clyde, then Manuel Lawrence,
Who cracked rattlesnakes like whips
And played hindcatcher without a mitt.

Manuel was the one who pooh-poohed
Space, cackling maniacally at the very mention
Of *the last frontier.* Anyone could see,
If you could go through it, it was not an end.

Beautiful Child

Because I looked out as I was looked upon
(Blue-eyed under the golden corm of ringlets
That my mother could not bring herself
To have the barber shear from my head),
I began to sense, as adults approached me,
That hunger a young woman must feel
When a lover seizes one breast too long
On the ideal nipple-balm of the tongue.
When they lifted me and launched me
Ceilingward, I seemed to hang there years,
A satellite in the orbit of their affections,
Spinning near the rainspot continents
And the light globe freckled with flies.
I could smell the week-old syrupy sweat
And the kerosene of many colognes.
I could see the veined eyes and the teeth
Dotted with shreds of lettuce and meat.
When I touched down, one of them
Would hold me to the torch of a beard
And goose my underarms until I screamed.
Another would rescue me, but leave
On my cheek the heart-mark of her kiss.
So I began, at three, to push them away.
There was no ceremony and few words,
But, like a woman who has let a man go too far
And, in one night's moodiness, steps
Out of a parked car and walks home alone,
I came suddenly to my life. They
Did not begrudge me, but turned back
To the things they had done before,
The squeaking bed, the voices late at night.
Mornings I'd crawl beneath the house,
Dreaming how poignantly tragic my death
Would seem, but, having thought about it,
I happily took myself into the darkness
Of the underground, where I was king.

First Space Travelers

Now that the future we believed in is history,
Where did we think they were going out there
Once the command modules of the early starships
Had been clearly revealed as paint and papier-mâché;
And the outer shells that rushed through granular stars,
Shapes cribbed from any lawn, mushrooms
Or milkweeds, a ruse like any grade-school operetta
Replete with wired costumes of spiders and worms,
And the old graveyard-defying heaven, the beasts
And the plots of ancient thrillers behind it all?

Our mistake was thinking that they had ever been born.
Today the dog barks, the telephone rings.
We have to live in the present, which is a gift,
And all the time, some fiduciary oracle
Implores us to hurry, with the earth sick of men
And the sun going out in ten billion years;
To save this, invest in that. I am just one man,
And that means I have a mother and a father,
Many things have passed, and it isn't history either,
Which requires vision. I'm not born yet.

But you should know there was a city
Thirty miles from home, designed by Henry Ford
For the workers of a mammoth auto plant that never was,
A place of graded and paved blocks
Where no one lived, no one lined up to miss
The parade that didn't pass, no one drove
Down quiet streets on mornings in late June
To the unbuilt harbor where the boats weren't docked.
Only the teenagers came there late at night
For drugs and sex forbidden to them in town.

You could see it, as the trees took it back,
If you knew where to look, as you passed over it
In a plane, the faint darkness among the green.
As a child, I remember wondering

If that is how it would be, the plans ripening
And souring, half realized, and the elders,
Who we had placed so surely in the past,
Hobbling ahead to the grave; was the future
A meadow where we would be laid out
Side by side, like books faceup on a table?

How would the story that goes on concern us,
Its never-never land, its once-upon-a-time
With deep space and stars and the frightening
Aliens with immense brains and sucker cups
Like medallions lining their feet and arms?
Who could I ever ask? I liked to lie on my back
Looking down into the sky, infinite and blue,
And then back up to the ground, sticks and rocks.
A cardinal burned low on a limb. I thought
If I were simple enough, it would sing for me.

Mink

It would come in the night up from the oil tanks,
Set like batteries on their scaffold by the barn,
And pause beside the outhouse, testing
With its preternatural nose the living dung
Before skulking on up the hill in the shadow
Of the grapevine and, for a second, freezing
Under the rotted eaves of the congested shed,
Listening deep into the shepherd's dream,
Before beginning, with the *skritch, skritch*
Of paws, to sink its tunnel under the sill,
Then rise among the hens brooding on their boxes
Of straw, while the boy and the girl lay
In the trembling premonitions before sleep,
In a room not more than thirty feet distant
From the thing they heard now as convict,
Mad dog, and conviction of the spirit.
So they would hold the silence in their mouths
And imagine the sun come to that same place,
Gilding pastures and fields, turning the roofs
Farther down the valley into ponds,
Each house white against the yellowing green
Of its quarter-mile kingdom, one after another,
Fainter and fainter in the distance
To the creek, which, in April, would spread
Brown silt on the fields and cover the road out,
So the wagons would have to go along the side of the mountain
By the old logging road to get to town,
And in a few more minutes the blackness
Would bring the morning on its shoulders.
They would run to the chicken house
And bring back the hen, inviolate except
For the twin blood marks of its fangs,
And, in time, the brother, as he waited
In a hotel bed, in the city of Minneapolis,
Would see a woman take it from her shoulders
And lift it over her head, so it would be
Clear to him, and he would know it by its name.

First Coca-Cola

Maybe a sin, indecent for sure — dope,
The storekeeper called it. Everyone agreed
That Manuel Lawrence, who drank
Through the side of his mouth, squinting
And chortling with pleasure, was hooked;
Furthermore, Aunt Brenda,
Who was so religious that she made
Her daughters bathe with their panties on,
Had dubbed it "toy likker, fool thing,"
And so might I be, holding the bottle
Out to the light, watching it bristle.
Watching the slow spume of bubbles
Die, I asked myself, could it be alive?

When they electrocuted Edwin Dockery,
He sat there like a steaming, breathing
Bolt, the green muscles in his arms
Strained at the chair's black straps,
The little finger of his right hand leapt up,
But the charge rose, the four minutes
And twenty-five hundred volts of his death,
Which in another month will be
Thirty-five years old. So the drink fizzed
With the promise of mixtures to come.

There it was. If the hard-shell
Baptists of Alabama are good and content
That the monster has died, so am I.
I swallowed. Sweet darkness, one thing
Led to another, the usual life, waking
Sometimes lost, dried blood in the ear,
Police gabbling in a strange language.
How else would I ever gauge
How pleasure might end, walking
Past midnight in the vague direction
Of music. I am never satisfied.

Letters from the Earth

The summer of polio, they drained the pools. I dreamed of Jehovah
Rearing from a *Pageant* magazine décolletage of Gina Lollobrigida.

My father, after riding through the fields masked like a bug, came in
With DDT caked on his neck and clogging the creases of his arms.

Salvaging the crops, leafing the pond silver with dead bream.
For weeks the beautiful Messiah of his cloud blew over things.

Certain insights may come only in childhood while reading Twain.
The hawks may come back only once from their near extinction.

At revival, Sister Melva, the evangelist-aviatrix, dispensed tickets
To children who repented, then took them with her up into the sky.

As I hung just above the ground, my legs hooked in a flat whitewall tire,
Aunt Brenda approached me, and asked, "Have you been saved?"

Later, knocking a baseball around in my grandparents' front yard
And feeling the urge to pee, I rushed straight in to the bathroom

Only to find Sister Melva, rising modestly from the commode
And wiping herself modestly with a white bouquet of toilet paper

That dangled one bedraggled petal onto the linoleum floor.
Like the light at Damascus, the white cheeks stared at me.

I knew nothing so shameful had ever happened before
And would not happen again. I stood there and bumbled out.

Certain insights remain fresh, where the world turns truest —
Truth's adamant like a tree. It only listens. It doesn't speak.

According to the laws of moral nature, proclivity for sexual action
May rise or fall in relation to the proportions of guilt to pleasure,

So childhood passes, and in time, many may come to goodness
With all the avuncular hubris of sexual memory turning into advice.

Since Darwin it's been the same with thinking people in the West:
The light of the mind, the darkness of the God.

Passing the old sanctuary, I think how, only once, I'll enter again.
Let them think of me burning, if that is what they want to believe.

The caught and the uncaught, we're going to one place —
They'll pray over us, and then they'll stick us in the field.

First Fraudulent Muse

Not seventeen, she dumped me.
No one has to tell me
A thing about the sorrows,
Aches, indiscretions,
And calamities of young poets
Of the United States
In the late twentieth century.
The poem I wrote then,
The one that would make her
Want me, either for my wry
Sensitivity or the scholarly erudition
Of my heart, is not this one.

It made some obscure reference
To the goddess Diana
While drizzling bad terza rima
About some poor decrepit wino
Eviscerating a garbage can.
My good friend looked at it
And made me know what
Kind of damn idiot I sure was.
His maxims come back — *read*
Everything, love language, revise,
Abide in the transforming fire —
And hers, mutated by distance.

While I was attaching the syllables
Of a certain mulberry tree
To an adjective that I loved,
She went and married an electrician.
Still I had to make a living,
Mindful of the preserving
Potential of the art,
And language clattering
Onto the platen like the small
Dark horse of the embalmer's salt.

Always it is the same night
I called her lily of the valley
And named her in many songs.
She keeps turning
Her cold beautiful shoulder
Into someone else's words.

II.

The Troubles
That Women
Start Are Men

In the Spirit of
Limuel Hardin

This morning some bald and wiry spirit,
Wreathed in smoke and shedding dark peals
Of laughter, has come down from the stand
Of cedars to hold forth to my father and me

Before retreating back into that soldery mist
Lifting above the portable sawmill.
Born the same year as my father, he is just old
And dying of emphysema, there is not enough

Breath left in him now to move the wing
Of a butterfly an inch from the scattering
Of chips cast by the blade of the saw,
But he laughs anyway, the laughter like

A fire that you draw up to, cupping your hands
And waiting for some ancient raconteur to squat
On his haunches and grub in the mulch
For a root to whittle into a box turtle

Before going on about the patient business
Of constructing oral history, but this morning
It is my father hemming and hawing
In that deliberate style that has marked

All his words since his stuttering childhood.
In his tale, everyone is dead or dying:
The Wilcutt girl, shot by her estranged husband,
After he returned, out of his mind on dope,

And held the family hostage, the sheriff
Talking to him all night, convincing him
To let out the baby and the grandparents,
But then the silence, the scream, the shots;

This is supposed not to make us laugh,
But I laugh, and then Limuel gets started,
A dry chuckle at first, like a shaft turning
In the crankcase of a rusting Farmall,

And you can see it hurts, but my father
Cannot stop. Now it is the Pruett boy —
He had just moved here, he was working
Behind his mama's house with a bulldozer

Leveling the thicket for a trailer pad —
That boy had always been afraid of hornets.
Right up under that big walnut tree
Where the old outhouse used to stand,

Suddenly the hornets on him like a blaze,
He jumped, and a woman working nearby
Said that the track rolled over his head,
No one could find it, though she got there

So fast, his hand still gripped a cigarette,
A long ash, and the smoke curling up.
Sad, my father says, and nods,
But all the time, Limuel and I, grimly,

Secretly, holding it, and now it comes,
The full-blown, gut-wrenching laughter,
The first hack, another and another, until
It has him on his knees in the wood chips,

Raising the inhaler, rubbing away the tears,
So we go over to him and help him to his feet
And walk with him as far as the spring,
And he goes on up into the trees, laughing.

Risks

I had not seen how dangerous the country was
Until he gunned it, downshifted into third,
And split the seam between the station wagon
Going east and the tractor-trailer going west,

The needle dead on the speedometer's horizon,
All of us tarred black from a day of laying pipe,
The cold Buds like tickets in our greasy fingers,
Him hollering fuckers and us begging stop

You son-of-a-bitch Jimmy stop this thing let me out —
We were going to college, we would be something,
And nothing like him, married, a dad at seventeen,
Though later, when we talked, it would be of him,

Stumbling home drunk at five A.M. to sucker-
Punch his father-in-law, then torch the garage,
As earlier, it had been of him, bolting from the cliff
Above the rock-crusher, clowning through flips

For the first fifty feet, then knifing down clean,
The water so smooth, and him holding his breath
So long down there they said there was a cave
Under a big rock where he would come up,

Roll a leviathan joint, and smoke it as we stood
Arguing the details of calling the rescue squad,
And then he would surface with that same hard
Contagious laugh he had carried from childhood,

As he had always been the one holding it up to us,
The tattoos, the muscles, the slicked-back hair,
Sassing and taunting, even when he had gone
To Nam and the dozen shit jobs and the pen,

After the burglaries, the assaults, the homicide,
Him talking through our mouths, him clenching
Our fists, him never taking it from anyone.
And now — given the consecutive lives to think,

The nights in the cell, the days sewing wallets,
Pressing sheet metal into tags, loading laundry
Into chutes, hoeing the prison beans — does he
Think of us at all, is he even conscious of us

When he dreams he has us begging on our knees?
And when the blood starts, does he love us
Now that we speak of him often and always
With that sweet fear that marks our liberty?

The Plan for World Government

Stiff on his new polymer knees, he comes across us
Rummaging through costumes in one of the hovels
That he's erected as part of his hybrid Bethlehem-
Gethsemane that works as a backdrop to the crèche
And passion play he's coordinated on top
Of the mountain each year since he left the ministry.
He seems so gentle and helpless, greeting me,
My wife must think him nice, if only a little odd,
As she looks up from a manger of wired halos
And tinsel stars and takes him in, a wizened man
Farmwork has burled and kinked like a knot.
But madness filled his cup those years he'd hold up
Sunday lunch by praying fiercely for half an hour
Against the godless, bootlegging Kennedys
And the satanic communists of the NAACP.
It flowed from the main tenets of his creed:
That the children of Israel had murdered Christ,
And marched in lockstep with the Russian bear;
That the children of Cain were that black family
Distributing poison whiskey just over the ridge;
So even now I think a fire must start for him
In my wife's accent and the shadow of her skin.
Well, shouldn't I pity him, studying each night
Some fresh light on the Book of Revelation
Or listening to xenophobic idiots on the radio —
Or perhaps I only imagine this from the times
When I've driven across the country hearing
The whole passionate chorus of men like him;
Or the days in pawn shops when I've read
The bulletins taped to the glass of gun cases:
Defend arms! Resist the plan for World Government!
But I remember the vise of his grip and how
He used to pick me up and swing me by the ears.

The Gift of Tongues

Recruiting field hands at the meeting at Powell's Chapel,
My father led us through the bluster of cussing men
Up into the sanctuary where the services would
Soon commence. It was like a box, cluttered, very

Hot, and everywhere potential hands worked fans
Like wings feathered with crucifixions. Then two men,
Their hair slicked back by lard, stepped up to the platform,
The first to read a text from Ezekiel which the other

Would then repeat because, he said, though he did not
Have the gift of reading, he had been called to preach,
Whereon the general whisper rustling underneath
Would cease, retreat to the back bench,

And come back in a steady fusillade of amens.
I sat there stunned by my first real smell of whiskey,
And then the preacher began to speak of the God
Who'd brought down fire on Sodom and Gomorrah

And given his only son that we might have eternal life.
He said the world might end tonight.
But first, listen to the testimony of Brother Mills.
He staggered in, a shaky man

Who plugged in an old Silvertone guitar.
While the feedback died, he allowed how we'd have
To pardon him. As many at the meeting knew, just
Two weeks ago, he'd been stricken with a heart attack.

He was back because of prayer. "Behold miracles!"
The preacher cried, and a fever of susurrations
Rippled the crowd. But Brother Mills, still shaky,
Eyes spangled with tears, declared: "I'm not a man

Of words; my testimony is my music," followed by
Three barely recognizable chords, two tunes:
"White Christmas" and "You Are My Sunshine" —
Next came the preaching: a host of demons,

Plagues, the bloody history of the Philistines.
At last, the common prayer, when all stood up,
Wringing hands and gabbling the unknown tongue,
Aya hunga ladooly majusta grizponk shifeely laboom,

Until I felt like joining in. But already, so long
Past bedtime, the noise was fading into my sleep.
And my mother was lifting me from the car.
The next week in the field, a boy would taunt me,

"If a rattlesnake was to bite you, you'd die right here.
But I wouldn't die. I've got the Holy Ghost."
Holy? Ghost? — I thought how I might answer,
And then I threw a rock high across the fence —

My on-the-spot cross of diplomacy and Zen
When I might have said a harder thing. Didn't
I know then, that sacred presence by which he lived,
That mean idiot in heaven was not my father.

The Troubles That
Women Start Are Men

On the porch, unbreeched shotgun dangling
Across one arm, just after the killing,
The murderer, Billy Winkles, made polite
Small talk with my father while we waited
For the sheriff to come. The reek of cordite
Still loomed above the sheeted corpse, his uncle
Ben, whose various dark and viscous organs
Jeweled the lawn. "Want some coffee, Von?"
I heard, and thought, A man is dead. And then:
Why had my father brought me there to stand
Alone, out of place, half-terrified, bored
With the slow yammer of weather and crops?

I stepped carefully across the rotted planks
Toward an oak where an engine block
Depended from a blackened limb and watched
A dull dazzle of horseflies, a few puddles
Hounds had dug like chocolate ruffles
Hemming the chicken yard. "I told the son
Of a bitch, come back, I'll shoot you dead,"
And he sure had, for sniffing round his wife.
He said, "It just ain't right." He rolled
A smoke and dragged a steady flame alive
While neighbors shyly stomped from pickups
And lifted the sheet to poke and peek.

"That's Ben," one said. "That's Ben to a T."
But was it? Was any of it real, the empty
House, the creek? My father saying, "Now
Your mother, she was a Partain, wasn't she?"
"Naw, she was a Winkles, too. My wife was
A Partain, she's over at Mai-Maw's now."
It went like that, and this. The wind drove
Up and set the shirts to popping on the line.
A red tricycle leaned above a one-eyed doll.

The mountain's blue escarpment unwound
Green bolts of fields, the white shelters
Where we lived, all of it somehow wrong,
And magical not to have changed while
Trucks backed up along the ditch and men
With their grown boys clambered uphill
To gawk at Uncle Ben who lay like shortcakes
Lined up on sawhorses on decoration days.

How strange, I thought, that no one prayed,
And strange that I was there, actually there,
With grown men, not sad or happy, but proud,
Knowing even then, the years would mostly
Amount to sleep, my father would come back
As history, and still there would be
To say the strobe of the ambulance light;
The sheriff, a tall, portly man, stooping
To help the handcuffed killer into the car;
And on the grass, bits of liver or spleen —
Whatever I'd dream, the world is not a lie.

A Slide of the Ladies Home
Missionary Society Meeting

When I get down to the bottom of things,
It was a dark green, stiff-billed soldier's cap
Stamped with the white numerals of one
Of the enigmatic insignia of the Alabama
National Guard. Why keep it now?
The boy who wore it, Billy Don Boulden,
Has been a man out of prison for a long time.

We used to play a fast hide-and-seek
In the woods just south of the house
Where the Ladies Home Missionary Society
Sipped iced tea as they watched slides
Of African children spraddling to scoop
Handfuls of ants into their mouths.
Just once I brought him, thirsty, inside

The house, and the good ladies, taking in
The darkness of his nappy head, looked
So aghast you would have thought one
Of the heathens had stepped down naked
From the white bedsheet they were
Using as a screen and now was debating
Whether to eat their earrings or their ears.

You know what it is to be *it*, don't you?
Since I drove up toward a cemetery
With a girl and we lay down half-naked
And rose up naked, with the horns blaring
And the long row of headlights shining
In our eyes, I've studied to memorize
The ground rules in the South: (1) God's

Watching all the time; (2) Every cemetery
Hides a church. It's always the same
With the two naked bodies, one moment
Alone in the darkness, and the next,
Two families in convention at the ten
Upturned toes. Mothers, fathers,
Grandparents, aunts, uncles, infamous

And demented cousins, like patriots
Appraising every possible outcome
Of every possible war, or certain
Familiar verses of the national anthem
That the singer cannot quite bring
To the tongue. The time machine
That changes the ludicrously tragic

To the mildly preposterous will arrive
In twenty minutes. If luck holds,
No one mentions marriage or pulls
A gun. But if you're fifteen and
Black, and a white game warden
Comes on you with a white girl
In the woods, in Alabama, in 1964,

One of the things that might happen
Is murder. If the white man's dead,
And you're caught in his car with a gun,
The jury takes less than an hour,
And you're building years, lollygagging
And jawing over the café au lait
In one of the bistros of Kilby Prison

Before the time machine turns into a bus
And lets you off with the night shift
Outside a laundry in Montgomery.
Old friend, I think of you running
A brush across some senator's pajamas,
Then of the slide, kicking into the light:
Somewhere in the Congo, circa 1959.

The ladies click their dentures into smiles.
King hasn't marched yet. We've
Just stumbled in out of the sunshine.
It's that instant when we're blind
And passing through the beam.
The feast of ants is painted on your back.
It's like all the past now. It's black and white.

The Pass

Longhaired in Walker County, driving
Home the week of Kent State, I worried
My green lid of homegrown marijuana.

This was deep in Klan country. There
Had been riots, bombs. George Wallace,
In three days, had called out the guard,

Then voided the semester. I drove slowly,
For the wind, the curves, and the coal trucks
Erupting unpredictably off side roads

Made the way perilous. For a few miles,
O. B. Emerson, that supremely delicate man
And epic bibliographer of Faulkner,

Rode behind me in his baby blue Firebird.
Then there was nothing but curve and hill,
With, once in a while, a semi looming

And descending to meet me in a blunt gust
That took and flung me to the side.
When a young man drives alone,

It is as if a faithful animal holds the wheel
While he draws from the bounty of his ego
The wishful story of his life to come,

A saga of martyrdom and nudity, recited
By Sir Ian Fleming in the alternating
Prose styles of Henry Miller and Henry James.

I thought my life would pass in erotic gentleness
And secret acts of philanthropy and heroism.
Then the old Plymouth swerved into my lane.

It wobbled, righted itself, and, dead
On my bumper, veered, bucked sideways,
Then flipped once before rolling

Behind me and vanishing in the pines.
I slowed, looked both ways, made a U-turn,
And pulled over in the grass. The wreck

Lay on the driver's door. The man inside
Groaned out to me. "Honey," he said,
"Get me some help," and I went running

Through needling briars. The ambulance
In Cullman was not twenty minutes away.
At the road, already the accident vultures

Were piling out. Then I saw him bending
From his car. "Dr. Emerson," I cried,
And a two-hundred-pound matron had his arm.

In those days, my friends and I worshiped
The accident, the joke. Each time we tripped,
Something would happen — a dwarf might

Stagger by, dragging a snarling Chihuahua
On a jeweled leash, or a row of mirrors
Would topple from a truck — so we'd feel

We'd tapped the mother lode of the absurd.
So the doctor explained himself, and roared off.
Back toward the wreck, I followed the crowd.

Three farmers had the hurt man like a rope.
"Wait," I said, "don't move him. What
If his neck is broke?" And one said, "Damn

Hippie, we can't just let him lay there
Sufferin'." Very gently, they drew him out.
Then he found me. "Honey," he said,

"You come back. Come over here a while."
I leaned down. "Closer now. There,
There." He smiled, and now he got my hand.

Not *that*, I thought, but this was getting odd,
The way he winked and swallowed long,
Nothing I could swear to, but the manner

Of it all, so I felt somehow I'd blundered
Into the gravity of a myth that wasn't mine.
Around us, the leaning faces made a wall.

Until the ambulance arrived, I'd sit there
Frozen in that thorny palm like a woman
Struck down in a field and ravished by a god.

A Ride with the Commander

Suddenly, in the back of the boat, my Quinn of Mexico cap blown off
    and shrinking
Behind me in the wake as we motor across the gulf, I look up
    to my father-in-law
Hunched at the throttle the way he must have concentrated years ago
    as he slanted from clouds
To dive-bomb a destroyer. I think, Just let it go, don't mention it,
    but then
He turns and, with his trained eye, gets a glimpse of it, bobbing back
    there like a duck —
And then me, bareheaded: "Well goddam, why didn't you tell me
    you'd lost it?"
By which I think he means not just the cap but how I've lived my life,
    so undisciplined and regardless
Of money that why his daughter puts up with me he'll never know.
    Maybe this is why
Now he jerks the boat so sharply that I'm slammed against the gunnel
    before he gooses it with
Such precision that by the time he cuts the gas and idles alongside,
    I'm sitting exactly where I was —
"Well, dip it out!" he says, and already as I snatch it, we're planing up
    to the speed he loves,
The maze of mangrove canals behind us, the Pacific calm in the distance,
    but choppy
In the bay's mouth, thundering as it masons its great white chimneys
    above the shoals,
So just as we turn, I imagine the night sky lit with fire, and life risked
    in terrible joy.
Another mile, we're gliding silently into the cove, and then, anchors
    down, we're as we were:
Me sitting with the women, digging in the warm sand for clams,
    and him frisking
The icebox for a beer before wading out to stand in deeper water
    with men like himself,

Men with large voices, bankers raised in the depression, merchants
      who have known war.
You can see this from the way they congregate equidistant
      from each other,
With their arms folded across their chests in equal poise — each
      has a secret
He would not divulge under any conditions, no matter the torture.

Indian Turnip

I wish the May apple would tell me what happened to Carl Peterson,
For it is supposed to be magical as it comes up from the swamp
And opens a green umbrella from the stalk of its toxic root.
It looks like a root my father gave me in 1971 —

Indian turnip, he called it, and told me hold it on your tongue,
Which I did, while the burning rang like a thousand needles
And a thousand telephones, and when finally I spat it out,
He could not stop laughing. He planted one in the back yard

By the pecan, but I do not know what happened to Carl Peterson.
One day he was talking, and then a shadow stood where he stood.
I know he went north, as everyone who vanishes vanishes north,
As I went north, and might have died, as some said I had died.

The last time I was home, a man looked at me, and said,
"I heard you was dead," but I looked at myself and I was alive.
But I do not know what happened to Carl Peterson.
For a while, I kept up with him, when he lived near Ithaca,

And I lived in Greeneville, Tennessee. Then for a few years
I had a friend, she worked for the government, she would look
Him up in the government computers, you are not supposed
To do it, but she did it, but I do not know what happened

To Carl Peterson. In 1978 he made sixty thousand dollars.
The checks were issued in New York State, but then a blank.
Perhaps he goes by another name, Peter Chomski or Carl Levine,
As the Indian turnip is also known as the jack-in-the-pulpit,

As the May apple is also called the manroot and the mandrake.
It grows also here in Illinois, for today I saw many as we
Walked the cliffs on that road that the state closes
Every spring to let the snakes migrate peaceably to the bottoms.

Today there were no snakes, only May apples, everywhere
We turned, there they were, and a friend there with me said,
"Probably the only signs of spring that do not stand for Christ,"
So I thought tonight I would look it up in the field guide

To see who used it in what potion or panacea and if religion
Or ritual was involved, though already it is past midnight.
Of course, it will not happen, forgetting is the work of sleep
And what use to remember gods who are nothing to us now.

The Consolations of Poetry

How many mornings, coming down the hall through the parked
    wheelchairs to find the old man dozing
Like a newt among the flowers, I thought of "Ozymandias" and
    "Endymion." How many afternoons,
Hearing the babbling and howling from farther rooms, I thought of some
    nameless song of Coleridge's
Or the things that John Clare wrote and that the young poets made
    a great stir of memorizing in the late seventies.
When the old man would wake up, wondering where he was, raving
    for a few minutes before
Wringing the dry ulcers of his hands, blinking and demanding his
    eyedrops, there were the few poems of Christopher Smart's
That someone picks up now and then, in the odd lucid intervals
    between television programs,
And thinks how true they are before going in to gorge on pesto and
    salmon. At other times
Seeing the ones with tubes down their throats, I would think of
    "Lycidas" and "Tamburlaine."
Sometimes one of them would make a noise, a shuddering really.
    It was not human;
It was like the noise a beast makes, like Grendel's vibrato down
    the abyss, like the souls
Of murderers in Dante, or the bull of heaven wailing the earth open
    in "The Epic of Gilgamesh."
It made me almost happy, there at the end, after the last few strokes,
    when the periods of speech
Had narrowed and grown further apart, to see how he had written
    down which measures would
Be permitted and which forbidden, so that he would die soon
    and no one else might profit from the suffering.
I would go out into the woods and study nothing for a long time.

III.

Close Relations

The End of Communism

Now I have Vallejo with me on the desk, his troubled words, and
        behind the words, his life tapped out
In Paris in 1938 while my grandparents shouldered one of the last
        springs of the Deep South depression.
Vallejo, who felt compassion for the travails of oppressed laborers,
        would not have imagined my grandparents,
Dirt farmers and slaves of nothing but survival, with no boss but
        cramping hunger and penury,
The work of a few mild days wedged between the cold spells and the rains.

They waged their revolution against clods, and when they'd dropped
        their seeds, the main battles were still to come.
The war against the weeds yielded to the long August drought —
        stillbirths everywhere, cholera in the wells.
Maybe my grandparents would have had no compassion for the
        suffering of poets, who, even then,
Had time to dillydally over huge books and learn foreign languages and
        skedaddle halfway round the world and live
In impoverished splendor while they bent their youths against the
        cheating fields.

But when Bird Wilheit came starving and broke, they let him sleep in a
        room behind the house,
For which privilege he was given the field beside them to work, a place
        at their table
And the luxury of living fifty more years, a slave's son and maybe a
        slave himself. My grandparents loved Bird Wilheit.
I do not know that they would have loved Vallejo for writing what they
        already knew, that the world was a thief,
That many murderers sat far away in the feathery chairs of heated parlors.

They knew that someone somewhere knew more than they knew,
        and that such knowledge,
Imperfect and querulous as it must have been, was more than tall
        cotton and no salvation.
They knew work started in the bitter dark and ended in the bitter dark.

They knew prices were fixed against them, and to hell with it
        as long as everything
They watered and pampered into life did not die of floods or drought.

I have done a little work with my shoulders, backs, legs, and arms. It
        has been a long time
Since I have done anything besides thinking, talking, and writing.
        What good is that
If it does not put a coat on someone's back? My grandfather, when he
        went into the nursing home,
Refused the government money. He was not rich, but neither was he
        broke. He worked.
Things came up. My grandmother moved beside him down the rows.

I do not know that anyone young will care what fomented the red dirt
        so I might fiddle with instruments
And read great books and mumble bad Spanish in my ripe Alabama
        drawl, but just because the shirt
On my back winds back to the drudgery of a field is no reason for guilt.
        I let the dead go on ahead of me:
My grandfather saying, "I reckon if you split up everything in equal
        parts, in five years the same folks would have it again";
And Vallejo reckoning "the enormous amount of money that it costs
        to be poor."

For My Sister

You will understand that the difference between us
In the volume and depth of voice had not started
To happen yet when I came from the woods
And saw you playing there the same as I would play

Except the games were different, the dolls, the house,
And not the guns but the endless bickering over roles,
The three of you, hands on your hips, always smiling,
Primping, or breaking, at odd junctures, into song,

But as with boys, the large owning the small. Never
Was I husband or father but myself, the little brother,
The one sent out to the store, the one you left behind
When you shopped in the attic, and came back to me,

In some shadow-cloven interlude deep in the afternoon,
Giddy with gossip and dressed in the ancient clothes.
Probably you would know the four terraces on that hill
I would run up and the pig wallow beneath the barn

Where I crouched and began to sneak toward the shack
Where the whore was admonishing her rotten brats
To come up from the pond and draw water for her bath.
It is even possible you had heard it was a brothel,

Though you would not know the inside of that place
Where we lived for years until the new house was built,
The open jars, the booze, and the music blowing out,
The whore screaming, "Goddammit, you little turds,"

And the seven of them hightailing it for the barn
Where I waited to be taught the rest of the dirty words.
I feel sure you will see the way it has always been
Down there, with everyone imagining the children

Will get the gospel straight from the cows, so it gets
To be girls talking to girls and boys talking to boys,
But the boys stood behind the girls. One of them
Said, "In the mornings, when it's cold, we got to lay

Under the bed and push. We got to crank mama up."
No one ever touched, but late one afternoon a bald man
I had seen in town came running out the front door
With blood clotted on his face and his shirt on fire,

A thing that, in all innocence, I meant to confess to you
As we sat together on the screen porch shelling beans.
I do not have to tell you whom you would have told,
For from the beginning we had been taught that part

Of the difference is nurture, and another part silence.
As our bodies grew into strangers, there were no words.
Only today after years it came to me that the shack
Had burned, and I thought you would want to know.

An Errand for
My Grandmother

The milk she kept under a ledge
In the spring, once lifted
To the light, would sour in a day.
That's why we have cows, she said.

But the green bubble-glass
Of the jugs might last forever,
She reminded me each time
I blundered up through the rocks

And back down to her jabber
And slab of chocolate cake.
Oh she was wise in other ways
But so old she appeared to be

Far behind me. I could not
Imagine her ahead of me,
Even when she came from the bath
And had me comb the long hair

Down her naked back, telling
Of the spring as it had been
In her own grandmother's life,
The Cherokees stopping there

On their way to Oklahoma.
Her own youth, how clear
It still seemed to her, running
And leaping, the same spring

I bring today to the blank page:
The cool water under the cool air,
And the mole above one shoulder,
The mint of a durable freshness.

Perfection

You who seemed not to have begun
To exist until I was born, only now
In my own middle age, seeing the house
Of your childhood, I begin to imagine

How it must have seemed growing up
There on the farm between the wars,
Up at dawn to the unceasing work,
Picking the cotton, pulling the corn,

With the beliefs arriving each Sunday
From the far-off history of the one book
And with only the one set of parents,
Like andirons, placed hard and stern

With everything depending on them
Until the tall shy boy who became
My father leaned to kiss you on the bus,
So it must have seemed a kind of end,

As if already a prince had lifted you
On his horse and spirited you away
To this house with its glossy antiques,
With its matching curtains and rugs,

And everything perfect, and nothing
The least bit rumpled or out of place,
Only the brilliance on the face of things —
One husband, one daughter, one son,

Like a studio's sample photograph
You take down and look at at times,
Saying, it was a life, it was wonderful.
But at first did it not seem narrow,

There in the valley with its one church,
And everyone thinking you stuck-up
Not to believe it all, the foot-washing,
The healing, the speaking in tongues?

Was it dull, pulling the heavy bucket
Up from the well, the outhouse cold,
The roof leaky, the halls dark and drafty
In those years before they ran the wires

With my father away painting houses
To clear the mortgage on the farm,
And you left to manage harvest alone —
Fierce and small, the cotton behind you

As you stood at the scales, weighing
The pick sacks, entering the numbers
In your perfect hand in the blue book.
That is how I remember you first.

Once when an ex-con from the hills
Tried to bluff you with a sack of rocks,
You dumped it on the ground outright
And banished him forever from the field.

Ground Sense

Because I have known many women
Who are dead, I try to think of fields
As holy places. Whether we plow them

Or let them to weeds and sunlight,
Those are the best places for grief,
If only that they perform the peace

We come to, the feeling without fingers,
The hearing without ears, the seeing
Without eyes. Isn't heaven just this

Unbearable presence under leaves?
I had thought so. I had believed
At times in a meadow and at other

Times in a wood where we'd emerge
No longer ourselves, but reduced
To many small things that we could

Not presume to know, except as my
Friend's wife begins to disappear,
He feels no solvent in all the earth,

And me, far off, still amateur at grief.
Walking the creek behind the house,
I cross to the old homeplace, find

A scattering of chimney rocks, the
Seeds my grandmother watered, the
Human lifetime of middle-aged trees.

Nell

Not until my father had led her into the paddock
And driven her a month in circles and made
Her walk six weeks with the collar on her neck
And the bags of seeds on her back did he snap

The leather traces to the hames, for she was not
Green halter-broke when he took her that way,
Rearing and shying at each birdcall of shadow.
It would be another year in blinders before she

Began seeing how it would go from then on,
Moving not as herself alone but as one of a pair,
With the sorrel gelding of the same general
Conformation and breed shuffling beside her,

And between them only the split tongue
Of the wagon. As is often the case with couples,
He the subdued, philosophical one, and she
With the great spirit and the preternatural knack

Of opening gates, they had barely become
A team when the beasts began vanishing from
The fields, and the fields, one by one, fell
Before the contagion of houses. Still, they

Were there for a long time after the first
Tractors and the testing of rockets, so you
Could see how it had been that way for years
With them, just the one motion again and again

Until at dusk when the harnesses were lifted,
The odor that rose seemed history itself,
And they bent to their feed in the light
That would be that way for the rest of their lives.

Filling the Gully

At the gully we park the truck
And start unloading — rusted
Mufflers, rotten barn timbers,
Shank ends of PVC —
A scoop at a time, stirring it all down
Through ruptured
Sandbags and the steam
Whelming up from the combustible
Heart of the wood chips.

Thirty-five years ago my
Angry young father got
Stuck here cultivating
The Johnson grass out of the spring
Cotton and, spinning in black mud,
Sank clear to the rear axle
Before giving up and putting on
His clean pants to drive
To the midnight shift at Wolverine Tube.

For three more rainy weeks
He had to leave the tractor there
With a tin cup over the exhaust pipe
Before he could get
His elderly team of half Percherons
And horse it out of the field,
But by then, already the gully
Was lizarding out of the rut,
Bottoming out and ending in sand.

Now my father is an old man.
When I come back in visits
One conversation deep
And three days long, I must seem
To him like one of those

Summer thunderstorms
That blows up out of the Northwest,
Makes its creek of muddy water,
And clears out by sunset.

I know he must ask,
What is my life worth?
A few poems, six lines
In the annual supplement
Of the *World Book Encyclopedia* —
When home is here — this farm
One hundred seventy years,
Our faces and the red loam
Furrowing over the same bones?

It wasn't me who worked the dirt,
So I hated it, from harrowing
To harvest, the hoe's glum
Ching off flint, abrasion
And claustrophobia of barns;
Hated even the fruit trees
My ancestors planted for shade
At eighty-yard intervals
Like stations of the cross.

Above us the sycamores
And the dark green hill of graves
Hunch like spectators
In some oddly silent stadium;
And still my father drives
The tamp down hard,
Steam spurting at his boots
As he buries the ruins —
Ten minutes, and it is done.

My Father's Memory

Back as far as he had it
In his head, he could tell
You everything about it
That you wanted to know.

If he had lived through it
Or seen it or heard it
From someone else. He
Could tell you exactly

The way it felt the morning
He found it. Whether
It was 1947 or 1923,
If it was a childhood pet

Or a tree, he kept it
If he had ever learned it.
He had not forgotten
Girls he dated, ships

He sailed on in the war;
He could show you
Clearings in the woods
Where houses had stood.

From a lump in the ground
He could bring up the body
Of a buried horse, the color,
Name, temperament;

Take him anything
Metal, shackled with dirt
And rust, he could tell you
Where it went on what machine,

Who bought it, who sold it.
If he had heard it once,
He still had the name for it,
And he knew it. He said —

When many came asking
To be reminded
Of things they had lost
Or where their people lived —

That was his gift. As far
As he could remember
He had never
Had a headache in his life.

Country Heroism

Noble Yokum was the Etowah county coroner.
The name seemed nearly ecclesiastical,
Linked, as it was, so often and intimately
With death by water, death by fire.

Mother had known him earlier
When he pedaled a black Schwinn down
The east pike delivering *The Decatur Daily*,
So I'd pepper her with questions —

"Noble had promise," she said.
"While others climbed fool's hill, he read
Fitzgerald and Thomas Wolfe — and one
More thing — you think too much of death."

"When I die," I told my mother, "shove
Me in a gully, and cover me with leaves."
I turned and huffed off to my room
To bury my head in the various falsettos

Rattling the chassis of my ancient Philco radio
Until the countdown shrank to number one,
And then, the burped-out, military tone
Of no instrument I could recognize

Would decrescendo to the news, which seemed
Like me and Edgar Allan Poe to favor
Mayhem — Noble Yokum repeatedly
Announcing the fruits of his investigation.

Those years I thought, once I'd renounced
Football and guitar, I'd practice law —
Professions my mother put no store in.
Surely being famous and living high

Were better than tending and slaughter.
Mornings my father returned from nights
Of pressing base tubes through the die,
And ate his eggs and read the paper

Straight through coronaries, murders,
And asphyxiations to Noble Yokum's name.
Mother shook her head. "What kind
Of work is that, declaring people dead?"

On Pickiness

When the first mechanical picker had stripped the field,
It left such a copious white dross of disorderly wispiness
That my mother could not console herself to the waste
And insisted on having it picked over with human hands,

Though anyone could see there was not enough for ten sheets
And the hands had long since gone into the factories.
No matter how often my father pointed this out,
She worried it the way I've worried the extra words

In poems that I conceived with the approximate
Notion that each stanza should have the same number
Of lines and each line the same number of syllables —
And disregarded it, telling myself a ripple

Or botch on the surface, like the stutter of a speaker,
Is all I have to affirm the deep fluency below.
The Hebrews distrusted Greek poetry (which embodied
Harmony and symmetry, and, therefore, revision)

Not for aesthetic reasons, but because they believed
That to change the first words, which rose unsmelted
From the trance, amounted to sacrilege against God.
In countries where, because of the gross abundance

Of labor, it's unlawful to import harvesting machines,
I see the women in the fields and think of how,
When my mother used to pick, you could tell
Her row by the bare stalks and the scant poundage

That tumbled from her sack so pristinely white
And devoid of burrs, it seemed to have already
Passed through the spiked mandibles of the gin.
Dr. Williams said of Eliot that his poems were so

Cautiously wrought that they seemed to come
To us already digested in all four stomachs of the cow.
What my father loved about my mother was not
Just the beauty of her body and face, but the practice

Of her ideas and the intelligence of her hands
As they made the house that abides in us still
As worry and bother, but also the perfect freedom beyond —
As cleanliness is next to godliness but is not God.

IV.

Elemental Powers

A Prayer to the Goddess

Mother of the ages, in all those years I was busy getting
And shedding religions, I never prayed to you for anything;
But the way the oaks just stood there, like great nerves,
Counseling the breezes to stillness, I wanted to ask them

What kind of thing I was. Also to commend them
For their generous forbearance in not reaching down
With their scrofulous arms and sucking me right up
Into their leaves. Couldn't I see they were hungry

And would have me soon enough, whatever I turned to?
Tiny and ignominious, I had just barely heard of relativity.
Earthly creator, if I had guessed you were feminine
I might have asked the warped cradle of the waxing moon,

But all I did was to turn back down the north slope
And descend, jumping from one side of the gully
To the other. There was my mother, frying chicken.
Pretty soon, my father entered in from the field,

And millennia would come and go, but not before
I fumbled my body to one girl in the back seat of a car
And drove through the countryside at a hundred twenty,
Praying to the stars to kill me or let her have her period.

I thanked the stones for their secret tenderness,
I praised the clouds for keeping their distance.
But how could I conceive of you, heretical presence,
Your breast clabbering the milky grass beneath my feet?

I throbbed to the adolescent systole-diastole, sex and suicide.
Confused as I was, I did not even know you existed
Except that the pith of everything worshiped and forbidden
Inspired some vague and unkeepable promise of the world.

The widows mumbled to you, as they trembled in the pews.
For a long time, I would go, too, on Sundays, and bow
To the palms and old man of that unimaginable heaven
Where the dead had much advantage over the living.

Sex

It was when I read Lawrence that I first saw the world
As a prime lushness, an opening not to be refused.
Wonderful hairs, wonderful mysterious equations,
Each hedge dripping, each clock breathlessly ticking
In the heat of that transcendent, pollinating clarity.
Not a rock or tree that was not suffused with it.
Every bug-ratty spiderweb a doppelgänger
For the flimsy verbal chiffon that revealed it.
Each sermon, each lecture, a wire that carried it
To where I lay studying it, if I studied anything
More resonant than the tiles on the ceiling.
For even as I smudged real numbers on a grid
Or traced vectors to a nexus of force and speed,
My mind kept struggling manfully to represent
Its infinitely compelling budding and lubricity.
And one morning Professor Nielsen said with regard
To my heroic inability to accept what was given,
Try to imagine a circle whose circumference
Is inside a proton, and whose center is everywhere.
I have thought of it long as a figure for desire:
A patent for the ridiculous, one of the paradoxes
The need for grace conjures up from lassitude and greed
Like a logical boulder or a Latin-speaking frog.
Often it takes the form of a vulva or a nipple
When it is not moonlighting with the physicists
As a black hole in one of those baroque cosmologies
That leads us like a big head through blinding insights
Until we end up bodiless in a mathematical field.
But as the boy I was grows distant, he seems
Not me but some antiquated piece of fiction
Expurgated from the years and quoted by testosterone.
Beef and ambition, fluttering under damp sheets,
He hums his soulful ditty to the sixth dimension,
And for a while the god in his britches brings him
The ambiguous miscellanies and etceteras of pleasure
Like bisque that comes on a flounder-shaped platter
At *La Lastra* in Puebla, a deep and pungent gruel

Alive in black olives, the crab leg indistinguishable
From the eye of the octopus, and all of it compounded
In many spices, like those prayers of penitence
The young Baptists weep onto the altar cloth
Less because they are admissions of guilt
Than because they are truly elegies for promiscuity.
Wonderful hairs, wonderful mysterious equations
I could confess, too, now, as my early lusts
Begin ossifying into greed. I could counsel
Abstinence. I know the sorry old man is sorry
For something. One night a woman
Came to me, not as a tree or rock, but in the one fire
Of her true life. What has that got to do
With anything naked in the naked faces of children?
This afternoon I am barely aware of the young women
As they jog over the bridge into Thompson Woods,
But someone must stand very still in the shadows,
Listening to the gusts that come just behind them
As though the veil of matter had been ripped
All the way back to the light of the beginning.
I hear it, too, fainter and fainter. Then darkness comes.
Why should I praise the exemplary life,
Possible only in age or failing health?
All that I love was founded on the same premise
As heaven: that pleasure lasts longer than death.

Dirty Blues

This young living legend leaning
Over the sink of the washroom
Of the Maple Leaf Tavern
Was not twenty minutes ago
Blowing the steel bolts out of
The twelve bars of "Stormy Monday."
Now I imagine he has
Come in from whatever
He kept briefly in the back seat
Of a buddy's parked car
To wash the fresh sediment
Of the flooding of the river Venus
From the skin of his prepuce.
Or is he just now anointing
Himself for some mystical
Communion to commence
Shortly in the scented
Cathedral of a stranger's mouth?
In a minute he will return
For the last set, the songs
So much alike, the women
Dancing with the women,
And the men lighting joints
In the courtyard where
The poet is buried. Just now
The way he goes at it
So carefully, from the tip
Back to the shaft, I think
He might be a stockbroker
Wiping a crust of salt
From the pores of a pair
Of expensive black wingtips
Before going in to purchase
Ten thousand shares
Of Microsoft. I know
It is none of my business
Where he comes or goes,

To what perilous conference
In the mean streets
Of the erogenous zones,
But I will tell my friends
Who wait at the oak bar,
Who will still be laughing
When again his music
Begins to darken inwardly.
This song he plays now
Is nothing but the blues.

Don't Worry

Most of us are compositions that begin in error
And curl like telephones in the umbilical swamp
And break into the light, rending the living portal,
And after long waddling, stagger to our feet
And after long goo-gahing, stutter into our voices.
Some would rather hear of Methuselah or Noah's ark.
A great many would prefer to meditate on springs
That slip right up from darkness unaware
And arrive, after much idyllic meandering, at the sea
Than imagine their fathers and mothers lost
To that act that often yields such indecorous mixtures
Of pain and pleasure we profane to call it love.

The talk that is only talk goes on talking its talk.
The priest talks to the pretty maid pregnant by a soldier.
She worries because there is war, or because soon
The war will be over, and there will not be
Enough work in the fields. The priest comforts her,
Saying, this too will pass, saying what priests say
In the name of the Father and Son and Holy Spirit,
As if each child came with a loaf of bread under its arm.
The professional grandmother counsels her granddaughter:
Get on with it, get it over, just don't marry a fool.
When my cousin went on the pill, my aunt inscribed
Letters to Billy Graham and Norman Vincent Peale.

Young, and risking car sex without a condom
Because the least trespass of sheepskin or latex
Against the glans seemed sacrilege against Eros,
When I arrived at that stage where the seminal vesicles
Begin to secrete their first milky pearls
And the girl there with me had at last vanished
Into the riptide of her own unstoppable motions,

I would think of mangled bodies at accident scenes
Or old men in Bermuda shorts with tar on their legs
In order to hold back the spasm of nearly intolerable pleasure
That was just my own spring, musicking itself
From beyond volition, like a violin in a cavalry charge.

Passing the clinic with a friend, I see a woman
Bow out of a taxi and move through the chanting gauntlet
Of fanatics raising their pickled fetuses, photographs,
And bloody flags. When one with a greasy
Beard and a ring in his ear darts from the crowd
And spits the word *murderer* right in her face,
My friend shouts back at them from across the street,
Something stupid and forgettable, to defend her
Who already has gone in to wait among the glossy
Plants and magazines, as though her own guilt
Had assumed palpable form and attached itself deep.
She sits there. It must feel almost as bad as being born.

What does a man know of *love?* His secret deliverance,
His blind spring joining the human river?
It flows darkly. It lasts as long as it lets him.
Because a man's immersion in pleasure stops
As it starts, he may spout bits of spasmodic wisdom
That seem leaked from the very plumbing of oblivion.
When my wife lay thrashing in the birthing room
Racked by the seventeenth hour of contractions,
And I passed a damp towel across her forehead,
I made the mistake of voicing the first words
That graced my mind, *I know just how you feel.*
She looked at me, and said, *You don't know anything.*

All My Children

Many poems I have forgotten, but never one breast
Hidden from me and just barely set in motion
By the delicate shifting from one topic to another
In our almost unconscious conversation.

Both of us knew, didn't we, what long
Troubles might start up between a woman
And a man, but there we were, late summer
Or early fall. We went on murmuring

While the Buddhists half a world away adorned
Themselves in flames. It happened then:
One of my shyly doddering thumbs found
A button, and she helped — sixteen years old,

God loves the world. I don't have to tell anyone
How it went, so that, years later, when I saw
Her once, pulling up at the self-service pumps
To fill her tank, I might have fainted, I hid

Behind an air compressor until she had gone,
But wherever I have gone, I have come back
And asked where she lives now and how
She gets along. I know she glides through

The country in an air-conditioned car and stops
At a farmhouse with busted shutters and enters
The fecal-smelling hall, passes under the flue-
plugging, pie-plate Jesuses. The old man,

Willowing with emphysema, looks up — Howdy,
He croaks out — and cranes his whole body to hear
Her running water in the tub, and she gets him
Under the arms and lowers him into the suds,

Frogs the warm sponge down the balding chest,
Body that might be my body, body
Of the world, gone flaccid and varicose — all
These poems, our children, should be grown now.

On Censorship

It is not going to disturb anything in the least
If I say to the brown wren that the bumblebee,
Who just a minute ago thundered by here like a bull
Whumping against table legs and the trunks of saplings,
Has gone and insinuated himself deep
In the spiraling black lace of the blackberry vine
And right now is sneaking a little poontang
Among the tender yellow labia of the buttercups.
To the squirrels, everything is clean. Say anything,
And they will not claw you or run you off,
And I do not have to elaborate and transcribe
Twenty-six volumes of the behavioral peccadilloes
Of our brothers and sisters the chimpanzees.

My grandmother, as she lay on her deathbed
In the Summerford Nursing Home, when
I mentioned that nothing was dirty, sat bolt
Upright and told me that the night her brother
Purvis died, he swore to her on three Bibles
He would not ever use bad language again in his life.
She said, "He accepted Christ and he died."
She looked at me hard.
Her eyes glazing like a clear stream
When a muddy stream running from a flood
Pours into it and the water begins to roil
And petal brown from the silt, she
Hung there like a fish in that holy place
Between the meaning and the word,
She cleared her throat,
And then she told it again, three times
The same story, and three different men.

I do not know what I could ever say
To make the iris, the foxglove,
And the painted trillium more beautiful
Than the whorled knots of cedar
And the mountains of southern Mexico.

I can't help the way I was brought up
To sit there and listen. I listened good.
My grandmother took my hand and smiled.
"You don't use that old bad language,
Do you, Rod?" "No ma'am," I replied.

For the last sixteen or seventeen years
I have been trying to describe what it is
About the female human genitalia
That makes grown men want to vanish
Into the woods and chew tobacco
Until they're dizzy and their hands go
Blue and numb with the cold.
They sit there in silence, thawing out,
Their faces burning and ringing,
And the gentlest of them sidle up
To the angry-looking heifers
And speak to them in low voices.
They run their hands along the muddy flanks,
And call them by the names of ancient
Wayward girls, "Delilah, Jezebel."

An educated person explained to me once,
"If you could translate Mozart into words,
I am convinced it would be positively filthy."
Big John Leeth said to me
More than thirty years ago regarding
The personal dignity and ultimate value
Of our work digging a ditch for that pipeline
Under the Fourteenth Street overpass,
"Taint — you know what taint is, don't you?
Tain't pussy and tain't ass."
When a young woman would pass
In short shorts or a skimpy top,
"Groceries," he would say, and lick his lips
And groan, "Umm Umm, them's groceries" —
But that isn't it either.

It is just an empurpled harp
Of fleshy folds hanging there at the bottom
Of the torso and almost hidden
In the silky or stiff mass of curls.
Even as it wets with pleasure
And seems to drive the mind
Deep into the dreamiest alcove
Of the last extinct bird,
It knows only the balm of touch,
But it is where we come from.

My grandmother's grave lies
Among the dark, largely unmentionable
Trees along the Holston River,
The black heron screeching up
There in the dead branches,
And the moon like that single lamp
Of the miner who will pick us
Out of the nearly invisible flux
And raise us up gold.

No one told her what loosened
Into her husband's tongue
Just out of her earshot,
That spate of indelicate oaths,
Organ sightings, and jokes,
But she must have heard something.
All her life, appropriating
The powers of silence,
She was no flower.

Hunger

I have never knelt to the earth and taken the crisp body
Of a beetle or the tender snack of an aphid on my tongue
And chewed it to paste and swallowed it down,
So I cannot speak of true hunger. One afternoon
In Alabama, Mitchell Tomlinson, who is an engineer now,
Offered me one of the dark gray lumps of clay
That he had been periodically stuffing into his mouth,
And I ate it. I am not saying it was good, but
I swallowed it, as if it were fudge. It tasted
All right, like salty creek water or the gunpowdery attar
That rises from a plowed field after a shower —
Only a little worse than boiled okra or collard greens,
And better than the greenish turtle egg I sucked
From a leathery shell on the beach one December afternoon
In 1984, and that wasn't bad either. I took it
Casually, the way, when I was very young, I would take
A woman in the vast inaccurate focus of my sexual hunger,
And, afterward, relishing the taste of her flesh and hair,
Would suffer no psychic indigestion of guilt.

If hunger has a body, it must have one eye that weakens
As its body grows larger. It passes over the stark
Beauty of the nearly starved. It has nothing to do
With curiosity, or the moment after a full meal
When a man enters the woods, and for no reason
That he can name, pulls down the nameless leaf
Of a nameless tree and chews it until the bits are so
Small that it takes ten minutes to spit them all out.
Sometimes when my wife and I walk near the house,
The huge boisterous dog who leads us around,
Marking trees, defecating in neighbors' yards,
Or greeting strangers by bringing the club
Of his nose up hard into their groins, will take
A nameless weed that way and chew on it a while
With such a flourish of scholarly concentration
That he looks to be one of the geniuses of intuition.
Up there on the mystical disk that spins in his skull,

He has all his hungers on file. They're like the footnotes
He consults at each mailbox and shrub, thinking
Them over very carefully and balancing everything out,
Before adding his own opinion and stomping off,
With his paws wheeling to tear up chunks of sod
And seal his codicil in the general territorial debate.
Hunger smells like nothing I will ever know,
But given my time on earth, I know to ask.

My wife says the worst thing she ever ate
Was *cocteles de concha*. A filthy woman
Would scoop them up from the fecal alluvium
That piles up in the shallow water beneath the pig wallows
And heaps of human waste that pour into the Pacific
Sixty miles southwest of the city of San Salvador.
With one hand, she would slice them from their shells,
And with the other, dice onions, cabbage, and tomato
Into the raw wound before squirting it all
With the juice of a dirty lime, and offering it to eat, barely alive.
It looked gray, she said, but she ate it, too.
I have no idea what mystery of the tongue compels us.
My wife won't say either, but she's had baby eels,
She's had bull gonads. She's sucked on pigs' feet.
That's our joke. Music of chance. Music of appetite.
We're like earthworms glowing in the dark. We know
Something unspeakable is running us through its mouth.

Bread

My grandmother's biscuits had the entire farm
In them — lard of the pig, milk of the cow —
And came from the oven, freckled as her hand.
The steam whelmed up then, salt odor

Of the very water that civilized our tribe.
Those biscuits, famous as thieves or arsonists
In our town, but so common as to be
Overlooked, were the one constant in her table's

Macaronian variations. My mother's biscuits
Were daintier, contrived, salvers of light
Dawning on the tongue, confetti of breakfasts —
Cat heads, my father called them. Praising

The flesh of those biscuits, he also praised
My mother's flesh and took it in his hands
Before us children, as he took those biscuits.
But I like *your* bread better, your sweet rolls,

And especially your loaves rising, the whole
House priming with the ale essence of yeast
Until one sits before us on its wooden board,
A clean sausage of the earth, crusted hard,

But tender underneath, like the true church
Hidden beneath the covenants and restrictions
Or a single oceanic soprano singing
Out of the ancient, moldy heart of Genoa.

But oh you would be blunt, and cudgel praise.
Now that you are away, that bread remains
Of all mixed blessings, that staff and club,
Dark golden and broken and perpetually sublime.

Lurleen

We're talking Bosnia and eating veal but also lasagna
My wife's tailored for my friend's vegetarian daughters,
A collage of asparagus, mushrooms, onions, and cheese.

But cheese — there's the hang-up for one, who's so devout,
Her father explains, she won't wear leather shoes or silk.
Pure she seems, but also gregarious, taking her salad

Like a bridge, devouring her cabbage and peas as the talk
Unwinds a ticker tape of gang rapes, shellings, genocide.
When she's aware that I'm aware of her, she smiles.

No need to apologize, I know, but the way she watches
The veal transmogrify across the table, I'm wondering
If there's not, in the fine relish of her dining, an assertion

Of distaste. She doesn't say a thing. She sees
The juice coursing down my chin. I'm eating
Proust and Galileo, but she doesn't chastise. She's quiet

And unreproachful, laying into a leaf as if it were not just
Mushy fiber, but the vital, incarnadine tincture of a feast.
Also I'm wondering if it's consciousness that makes

Her good. Aren't women, by nature, herbivorous?
So I'd thought: herbivorous women, carnivorous men —
A suspicion I'd be hard put to admit, reared as it was

From such a tenuous complex of things, a botched
Sense of history, mother's cravings for beans?
Didn't Socrates warn against the philosophy

Of young men — they had, he owned, such a narrow
Phalanx of particulars from which to derive generalizations?
But what I felt at her age, those paralyzing sensitivities

To lives opposed to mine, the universe condensed
In each cell, and my indifference in the face of it all:
Wasn't that real, the longing for holiness, and terror,

When it seemed a normal walk across a sticky floor
To answer a phone might kill millions, maybe billions,
Of microscopic lives, and one of them might be God?

Then there was the war, complicating judgment,
As now the wine begins to act on deeply plural whims.
Suddenly I want to blurt out everything I've killed

And eaten: rabbits, chickens, many fish, the sow
I'd named Lurleen for the governor's wife and raised
From a pig, things that seemed natural on the farm,

The killing and being killed, and knowing the names:
Important to know the things we eat, good or bad,
That is what I'd say to her of love. That or this:

"Lurleen," my father would say, "pass the Lurleen."
And I had an uncle, who as the cancer ate at him,
Began to love the cancer, even as he turned yellow,

Holding up the charts of his demise that showed
An alien thing going up like the wing of a cathedral
Before it took and whispered him up into the grass.

How innocently the desserts arrive, pale saucers,
Beautiful and sweet fruit, and the human afterlife
Wearing its grass to the ruminations of the cow.

Oh, my dear one, it watches us watching it.
We know, as it bends to the grass and lives,
The cow knows a few things that it's not telling.

After Workshop

To write lucidly of a broken engine, a comical funeral,
A bad marriage, or flooding street, surely there must be
Some good in all of that. Then to stand at the bar

And know the unrevisable world, the television on,
And a dozen working men shouting at the game,
From which one woman turns in a parody of despair,

And proclaims the death of poetry. I think of Rilke,
That he should live, in the scuff marks breath leaves,
Even in the translations of words I never heard spoken,

Carried on a river flown long ago into a sky no one alive remembers.
The voice is the fiber of the self and a dumb vessel
Loss has hollowed into a smooth instrument of pleasure.

Not that we will die less for having spoken frankly,
Even if it is no more than the style of a windowsill or door
Entered secretly in the whisper vault of an uncharted breeze;

Nor that the wind, as it declares its public secret
Would leave one signature in our flesh. We say
The things it has shaken, the nerves' clear compass,

The politics of trees, as though the ego's sly decorations
Would invite guests across the closed borders of years.
We will have to be more than words to take their coats

And serve them drinks and food, and yet must be words
Offered into the nature of things, as ashes float down
While the broom goes about its thoroughly ordinary business.

We must say the work of a usual day and the streets we know;
Must say, too, the extraordinary detonation that did not happen.
How could we have ever been a jot more than nothing

There at the rag and mischief end of history
If we did not bring back from the vision of that last day
Some remnant of the god who would go on beyond us?

The ideals frisked of magic, and words raining on things —
Who wants to hear them now, as the game ends and the ice
In the glasses spreads feathery coils of clarity, and a general

Shuffling to the bathroom announces the songs of love?
Stupid songs, but the songs everyone listens to after midnight,
The songs that make the poets sad, though two women,

Perhaps because they are drunk, come out of the shadows
And dance in front of the jukebox. Woven to each other,
They weave, slowly and bravely, promising immortality.

Waking Up

These were my worst nights, three A.M., waking to claws ravaging
      the garbage cans outside the mortuary,
Squawk-bleat of cats in heat, perdition's spit and hiss, and then
      the rending down through plastic bags
To the scavenging at the very core of things, a fierce, liquid gnawing
      of gristle fevered occasionally by competition,
And then gone, leaving only the room smeared with the unction
      of streetlights, a cheap vinyl couch
And matching chair, the one fabulous child asleep, and the woman
      I did not love, sleeping also,
The ventilation of her snoring like those slubs or rips craftsmen leave
      in the fabric to suggest the virility of error,
And then the birds, the red, many-ventricled machine of their clarity,
      first the male and then the female
At the ancient Ping-Pong of shrill territorial claims and bland
      warblings of adoration, which served as both
Aubade and counterpoint to my guilt, my doomed, unnecessary,
      hydra-headed guilt.

All morning, Melody, the teenage welfare mother across the hall,
      would plot with her social worker to come off the dole.
Drunk by midafternoon, ranting to her colicky child, "Shut up, just
      shut the fuck up, you little pig!"
She flung her red spike heels against the wall to make the pre-Depression
      plaster fall.
Twilights I walked, fog in a plaid shirt, reconnoitering among
      boarded-up hotels, dripping change
On the counters of grocery stores, and when I came back, a hearse had
      backed up to the side door of the funeral home,
The wood of the casket shining, and under it, the unimaginable body,
      the human lettuce of autopsies.
Many nights I came back to the house, wanting another life, and
      climbed the stairs to the three brown rooms,
And there it was, stretched out before me, and by God it was my life,
      and still it was not my life
The six black men bore down the gamut of last friendliness and slid
      into the hearse.

How untrue *I* was, how craven, not to have spoken of it, only to have
        drifted off on the whim of some half-ass infatuation:
Body of the instant, high cheekbones, heavy legs, dark African-
        Caribbean eyes, each night, the breasts
I lifted like mugs, the mouth's wet kiss, and Catholic cry,
        "Don't hold back" and "Come inside of me."
Stepping out on the path of wayward husbands, getting it on the side
        in the apartment of a friend —
And once, both of us drunk, crawling in the wrong window to find
        an old woman whispering to a scabby Pekingese dog.
Eyes pronating under the balding patch of skull, she trembled up like
        a lit match hollowed suddenly by the north wind. We ran.
What could we do but run? And laugh, as we ran past the living
        buildings, down the dead street,
And into the car, whistling off through the enormous, jasmine-scented
        night, darting between
The hills of the Holston River to finally light on the black leaf of a
        parking lot.

My worst nights, how incredible and flimsy you were, kindled from all
        the brevities, as though the cremation to come
Were but one instant among the infinite years the gods we no longer
        believe in take to make love from human error,
Or as though the existing god were abandon and my life were another
        man's life that woke when I slept
And slept when I woke, until I heard the cats, and went over to the
        moonlight to see what was torn and mutilated.
I leaned out. I knew I wanted to live. What was my life, coming into
        focus above the toothed nucleus of the shadow?
It would take another two months, backbiting, slander, every kindness
        vanished, lawyers talking to lawyers,
But just then, before the settlement, there were the cats, their snarls
        balanced against their mouthfuls of meat.
Whatever it was, horror and ignorance. It would be important to love
        beauty, whatever beauty is.
It would take years. It might have been the guts. It might have been
        the heart.